Travis Air Force Base

The USAF's Transport Superbase in A⌐

SCOTT CUONG TRAN AND NICK TRAN

KEY Books

Back cover image: A massive C-5 prepares to land at Travis AFB with all 28 tires ready to touch down on the runway.

Title page image: A busy flightline: a KC-10 waits on the taxiway, ready for a refueling mission, as a C-5 takes off in the distance.

Contents page image: As seen from the top of a C-5, the ramp and airspace are chock-full of aircraft, including KC-10s, a C-17, and a visiting KC-135.

Dedication
To all the hard-working and professional airmen at Travis AFB.

Acknowledgements
The authors would like to thank all the airmen involved in the writing of *Travis Air Force Base*, specifically those who took the time out of their busy days to be interviewed and to show us their profession: A1C Monte; A1C Ramos; A1C Sanchez; SrA De La Cruz Rivera; SrA Galberth; SrA Hawley; SrA Hinks; SrA Pascual; SrA Sundin; SrA Trent; SrA Waller; SSgt De Leon; SSgt Jacobs; SSgt Murray; SSgt Rodgers; SSgt Sanford; TSgt Thomas; TSgt Valenzuela; TSgt Wood; MSgt Cubol; MSgt Foley; Lt. Oppenheim; Lt. Simmons; Capt. McNatt; Maj. Foley; Maj. Persico; Maj. Robinson; Lt. Col. Fisher; Lt. Col. McClintock.

A special debt of gratitude goes to Lieutenant Amelia Chromy and Technical Sergeant Levi Reynolds who organized a week-long tour of the base and escorted the authors around, keeping them out of trouble. All efforts have been made for accuracy, and any errors or omissions are solely the responsibility of the authors.

Published by Key Books
An imprint of Key Publishing Ltd
PO Box 100
Stamford
Lincs PE19 1XQ

www.keypublishing.com

The right of Scott Cuong Tran and Nick Tran to be identified as the authors of this book has been asserted in accordance with the Copyright, Designs and Patents Act 1988 Sections 77 and 78.

Copyright © Scott Cuong Tran and Nick Tran, 2022

ISBN 978 1 913295 79 0

Typeset by SJmagic DESIGN SERVICES, India.

Contents

Introduction

One of the most storied and important Air Force bases (AFB) in California, Travis AFB is known across the US Air Force (USAF) as the "Gateway to the Pacific" because of its strategic location and airlift capabilities. A part of the Air Mobility Command (AMC), the airmen at Travis are responsible for moving more cargo than any other base in the continental United States. Travis is located about an hour and a half drive northeast of San Francisco, in the sleepy town of Fairfield, and hosts the 60th and 349th Air Mobility Wings, as well as the 621st Contingency Response Wing. There are two main parallel 10,000ft runways, designated as 03L/21R and 03R/21L, with an additional 4,000ft assault strip for short take-offs and landings, aligned in a northeast/southwest direction. Assigned to Travis are 58 AMC aircraft and nearly 13,000 personnel, including 7,000 active-duty military, 2,700 reservists, and 3,300 civilian employees and contractors. As a complete base, Travis is also host to the Travis Unified School District, which enrolls over 5,000 students between kindergarten and twelfth grade (ages 5 through 18), who are mostly children of Travis airmen.

Travis AFB's mission is to project American airpower across the globe at a moment's notice, and they are able to do so with their cadre of C-5M Super Galaxy, KC-10 Extender, and C-17 Globemaster III aircraft. In 2019, Travis aircraft flew over 27,000 hours in 5,900 sorties, delivering over 24 million gallons of fuel in air-to-air refueling operations, and transported 22,000 people and 30,000 tons of cargo. Over 600 Travis airmen are deployed at any given time to various locations around the world, with missions ranging from providing medical care to Afghan refugees, ferrying helicopters and tanks to partner nations, and participating in kinetic operations with Army and Marine counterparts.

A rare view of all three aircraft types at Travis Air Force Base (AFB) in front of the control tower. From left to right are the C-17A Globemaster III, C-5M Super Galaxy, and KC-10A Extender.

Welcome to Travis Air Force Base! The sign outside the Visitor Control Center leaves no doubt as to who owns the base and the skies above Travis. (US Air Force photo by SrA Cameron Otte)

The logistical support provided by Travis airmen is unmatched by any other AFB. General Frederick Franks, commander of VII Corps during Operation *Desert Storm*, quipped "Forget logistics, [and] you lose," and without the supply lines produced by Travis, American military prowess would be significantly denigrated. Even the toughest special forces operator cannot sustain a fight without food and weapons, and AMC delivers those vital tools to the front lines. With over 100,000 Airmen and civilians representing nearly 20 percent of all USAF personnel, the Air Force knows that the AMC is its backbone for delivering important cargo. The influence that Travis airmen have on airpower cannot be overstated, as they allow for sustainment over vast distances.

At the outset of World War Two, the Luftwaffe made great gains by having a logistics system that was able to support an average of "four to six sorties a day, whereas French air force fighters only averaged one per day."[1] However, as their supply lines began to extend and campaigns became drawn out, their ability to provide cover for the Wehrmacht started to wane. In just two years after the beginning of the war, "less than 30 percent of the Luftwaffe's forward air units [in the Eastern Front] were operational," due to "the rigors of the campaign or [lack] of fuel,"[1] resulting in the Soviet military being able to push back and counter in late 1941. As a result of poor logistical planning, the Luftwaffe was unable

to generate enough sorties and was eventually beaten back. To avoid a similar failure, senior US military leadership places a high emphasis on moving supplies to the right places and is reflected in the high quantity and quality of personnel and funding furnished to AMC and Travis AFB.

This book highlights only a fraction of the capabilities and operations at Travis AFB. The authors were generously granted interviews with many airmen and access to the runway, aircraft, support facilities, and a flight on a C-5M. Information contained in this book is current as of November 2021. All images, except where otherwise noted, were taken by the authors with Canon 1DX Mk II and 7D cameras, with lenses ranging from 28mm to 600mm.

As seen from the cockpit of a Galaxy, a Travis KC-10 prepares to connect its boom to the refueling port on the top of the C-5.

1. Higham, R., & Harris, S. J. *Why Air Forces Fail: The Anatomy of Defeat.* Lexington: University Press of Kentucky, pp 207–208 (2016)

Chapter 1

History of Travis Air Force Base

World War Two

Travis AFB was initially built as an Army airfield in response to the attack on Pearl Harbor in December 1941 and was originally named the Fairfield-Suisun Army Air Base (AAB). Activated in May 1943, it was originally envisioned to protect the West Coast from a Japanese invasion, hosting medium bombers of the 4th Air Force, such as the A-20 Havoc, A-26 Invader, B-25 Mitchell, and B-26 Marauder, but its strategic location as a transfer point to the Pacific was soon realized, and the base was assigned to the Army Air Corps Air Transport Command. Fairfield-Suisun AAB was nestled between several other airfields including McLellan, Mather, Stockton, and Hamilton Fields, and was used as an emergency airstrip. One runway was even configured as an aircraft carrier, and the US Navy made great use of the base as well. Because of its close proximity to highways, railyards, and the San Francisco Bay, Fairfield-Suisun AAB was a perfect hub for inbound and outbound cargo, and it slowly became the main aerial port for the West Coast. The first host unit at Fairfield-Suisun AAB was the

This KC-10 shows off Travis' heritage as a former Army Air Field with its nose art. In 2018, Travis hosted a 75th anniversary event that included a golf tournament and a formal dining-in.

23rd Ferrying Group flying converted B-24 Liberators to transport men and materiel to the Pacific Theater, specifically Hickam Field in Hawaii. By war's end, Fairfield-Suisun AAB had established itself as the gateway to the Pacific for air transportation.

Strategic Air Command

In 1949, Strategic Air Command (SAC) assumed control of the base and began flying the B-29 Superfortress, B-36 Peacemaker, and B-52 Stratofortress of the 14th Air Division as part of its long-range bombing and reconnaissance mission. In August 1950, a B-29 carrying 20 passengers and an explosive payload crashed shortly after takeoff, killing 19 people, including Brigadier General Robert F. Travis. A popular commander, base officials petitioned to rename the base in his honor, which became official in October 1950. Travis AFB experienced its greatest land expansion under SAC, gaining over 6,000 acres. The 14th Air Division ended its stay in 1958, moving to Beale AFB and ending SAC's command over Travis AFB.

Air Mobility Command

Now a part of Air Mobility Command, Travis AFB has hosted the 60th Air Mobility Wing (AMW) and the Reserve 349th AMW since 1966. The 60th and 349th AMWs currently fly the KC-10 Extender,

Travis is home to 26 C-5M Super Galaxies, like this example. C-5M serial 84-0060 proudly displays its Travis banner, with the three chevrons as a nod to the 60th Air Mobility Wing (AMW) logo and the California flag.

The Travis flightline can be full of surprises. Aside from the usual KC-10s and C-17s, a visiting KC-135 is seen here on the left. Other frequent visitors include T-38s from Beale, which U-2 pilots use to maintain their proficiency.

C-17 Globemaster III, and C-5 Super Galaxy, which provide petrol, people, and pallets to the fight. Some other aircraft that the 60th and 349th have flown include the KC-135A Stratotanker, C-141 Starlifter, and C-133 Cargomaster. Travis is one of ten AMC bases, and the others are Grand Forks (North Dakota), McGuire (New Jersey), Charleston (South Carolina), MacDill (Florida), Dover (Delaware), Fairchild (Washington), Little Rock (Arkansas), McConnell (Kansas), and Scott (Illinois) Air Force bases.

A busy flightline is seen here as a C-5M takes off behind a pair of C-17s. Crews practice flying in inclement weather, and this rainy day was perfect for such training.

Out with the old, in with the new: a C-17 taxies past an old C-5A, which has been stripped for parts and is scheduled to go to "The Boneyard" at Davis-Monthan AFB.

The USAF roundel on the C-5M sits next to the Infrared Countermeasures (IRCM) laser, which is designed to confuse incoming infrared-guided missiles.

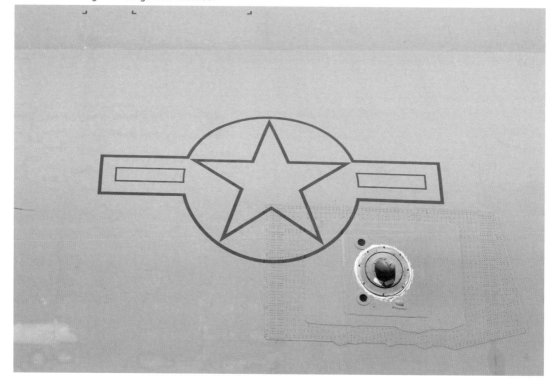

Travis AFB Aviation Museum

Celebrating Travis AFB's contribution to the USAF is the Aviation Museum, located in an old commissary. There are 22 static aircraft on display, such as the B-29 Superfortress, B-52 Stratofortress, C-141 Starlifter, and F-86 Sabre, with more aircraft scheduled to be added in the near future. Additionally, there are over 50 exhibits inside the museum that chronicle the history of Travis from World War Two to the present, while also exploring the base's contributions to space exploration and other humanitarian missions. One of the more impressive displays is in the engine room, where nearly 20 powerplants of all types are on display, including a rare Soviet Tumanski RD-9, a turbojet that powered the MiG-19. The museum also contains an extensive library with over 3,000 books on file, which are available for researchers to check out. There is also a fun gift shop that allows visitors to take home a piece of Travis and support the museum at the same time. Much of the work done at the museum is done by an army of volunteers who understand the value of preserving the heritage and history of Travis AFB. The museum director and base historian work hand in hand to ensure pertinent records are kept both for posterity and to help the base commander operate more efficiently.

Aircraft from various decades throughout the US Air Force history sit on display at Travis Air Museum. It holds organized displays of Air Force history, showcasing the Tuskegee Airmen, the Consairways story, the Berlin Airlift, and the history of Travis AFB with special emphasis on World War Two, the Korean War, the war in Vietnam and other significant military missions. (US Air Force photo by Nicholas Pilch)

Chapter 2

Current Organization

60th AMW Groups

The 60th AMW's motto is "termini non existent" ("there are no bounds"), and its three aircraft types ensure that there are, indeed, no bounds to providing airlift support around the globe. The 60th AMW is split into four groups: Operations, Maintenance, Mission Support, and Medical Groups. The 60th AMW staff includes other critical functions including the 60th Comptroller Squadron, Chapel, Inspector General, Historian, and Public Affairs.

The 60th Operations Group is the wing's flying group, consisting of the 21st and 22nd Airlift Squadrons (AS), 6th and 9th Air Refueling Squadrons (ARS), and the 60th Operations Support Squadron (OSS). The 21st AS flies the C-17 Globemaster III and the 22nd AS operates the C-5M Super Galaxy. Both ARSs keep the fuel flowing with the KC-10 Extender. Weather forecasts, training, and airfield operations are handled by the 60th OSS.

Six squadrons comprise the 60th Maintenance Group, including the 60th, 660th, and 860th Aircraft Maintenance Squadrons (AMXS), 60th Aerial Port Squadron (APS), 60th Maintenance Squadron (MXS), and 60th Maintenance Operations Squadron (MOS). Travis AFB's C-5Ms are cared for by the 60th AMXS, while the 660th AMXS looks after the KC-10s, and the 860th AMXS are responsible for the C-17s. Known as Port Dawgs, the 60th APS prepares cargo to be loaded and unloaded, including packing and rigging parachutes for aerial drops, loading cargo onto the aircraft, and securing cargo for flight. The Port Dawgs also perform inspections of cargo, ensuring that hazardous materials are stored and secured properly. The 60th MXS repairs and maintains the aerospace ground equipment vital to keeping the aircraft operational.

The crest of 60th AMW has three chevrons, symbolizing flight and the rapid mobility the unit is able to provide. (Photo courtesy of Travis AFB)

Supporting the Travis mission is the 60th Mission Support Group, composed of the 60th Civil Engineering (CES), Communications (CS), Contracting, Logistics Readiness (LRS), Security Forces (SFS), and Force Support Squadrons (FSS). Maintenance of Travis AFB is the responsibility of the 60th CES, which improves roads, repairs facilities, performs firefighting duties, and controls pest populations. Additionally, the Explosive Ordnance Disposal teams are under the 60th CES. Cyberspace capabilities are provided by the 60th CS, enabling worldwide communication. The 60th Contracting Squadron works with civilian contractors to provide services to Travis AFB. The 60th LRS is responsible for supplying, storing, and safeguarding inventory, including weapons, aircraft parts, and body armor. Base security is the responsibility of the 60th SFS, which guards the entrances and ensures prying eyes and ears do not get too close to sensitive equipment and information. Boosting morale and taking care of airmen is the job of the 60th FSS, which offers childcare, club activities, professional development, honor guard, and mortuary services to the troops and their families.

Serving over 500,000 airmen, veterans, and their beneficiaries across eight western states is the David Grant USAF Medical Center (DGMC), which is the largest Air Force medical center in the US. It is named after Major General Dr. David Grant, who helped found the USAF Medical Service, which gives unique medical care to airmen, such as treating post-traumatic stress disorder, brain trauma, and other combat-related injuries. The Department of Veterans Affairs has also integrated with the DGMC to care for veterans, enabling ease of records sharing and improved customer service. The DGMC is part of the 60th Medical Group (MG), which is comprised of seven medical squadrons performing essential functions such as dental, surgical, and inpatient operations. Personnel from the 60th MG have deployed to major conflict zones across the world, including Iraq, Bosnia, Somalia, Croatia, and Afghanistan, to provide vital and lifesaving care to military and civilians. Medical personnel from the 60th MG are experts in their field and demonstrate that by providing a bevy of services that rival any military or civilian hospital in the world.

Not one to sit on the sidelines, the 60th AMW has participated in significant operations since the end of World War Two, including the Berlin Airlift (Operation *Vittles*), the Gulf War (*Desert Shield/Desert Storm*), and the Global War on Terror (operations *Enduring Freedom/Iraqi Freedom*). The 60th AMW also participated in a record-setting around-the-world flight in 1995 by refueling two B-1B Lancers on their nonstop 36hr 13min mission across the globe.

There is no doubt who this KC-10 boom belongs to, as its unit is emblazoned on the underside of the flight control surfaces.

This logo clearly identifies this aircraft. The C-5M logo adorns all Super Galaxies at Travis.

Hard working maintainers prepare a KC-10 for flight. Note that the personnel are able to stand underneath the aircraft, shielding them from the elements, a feature not found with the C-17 or C-5.

349th AMW Groups

The 349th AMW is the Reserve component to the 60th AMW and is grouped similarly to include the Operations, Maintenance, Mission Support, and Medical Groups. The Air Force Reserve augments the active duty component by flying and maintaining the same front-line aircraft. Nearly 90 percent of the Reservists serve at least 40 days per year and are able to maintain civilian jobs. These "citizen airmen" are a key component in national defense, filling operational requirements when there are not enough active personnel to fulfill those missions.

The 349th AMW moved to Travis AFB in 1969, flying the C-141 Starlifter, and has been a part of every major Air Force operation, including the Vietnam War, Persian Gulf War, and the Global War on Terror. Additionally, the 349th AMW is keen on participating in the humanitarian mission, providing relief during Hurricane

The 349th AMW logo shows a wyvern delivering a paratrooper around the world, showing their ability to deliver men and materiel anywhere and anytime.

Katrina, the Loma Prieta and Northridge Earthquakes, as well as international crises such as the 2004 Indian Ocean earthquake and tsunami and 2011 Tohoko earthquake.

The 349th Operations Group has seven squadrons, with the 70th and 79th ARS operating the KC-10 Extenders, the 301st AS flying the C-17 Globemaster III, and the C-5 Galaxies being flown by

These airmen and their civilian counterparts are preparing C-17 06-6158 for a medical mission to Alaska.

Let's Roll! This C-17 embraces the "Spirit of 9-11," referencing the heroic actions of the passengers on United Flight 93.

the 312th AS. Rounding out the Operations Group is the 349th Aeromedical Evacuation Squadron, Operations Support Squadron, and Mission Support Squadron.

Keeping the aircraft in the air is the 349th Maintenance Group. The 349th AMXS, 749th AMXS, and 945th AMXS are responsible for the C-5 Galaxy, KC-10 Extender, and C-17 Globemaster III, respectively. The 349th MOS and MXS support the maintenance squadrons by ensuring they have the tools and parts they need to complete the job.

Helping the base and its residents is the 349th Mission Support Group. There are three Port Dawg squadrons: 45th, 55th, and 82nd Aerial Port Squadron. They are augmented by the 349th CES, LRS, FSS, and SFS.

The 349th Medical Group has three squadrons that help heal airmen and civilians alike. The 349th Medical, Aeromedical Staging, and Aeromedical Medical Squadrons work with the DGMC to care for wounded warriors and returning veterans.

621st Contingency Response Wing

One of the more interesting and unique missions in the Air Force is the concept of air mobility, specifically expeditionary airlift, which entails providing airfield capabilities in austere, remote, or otherwise suboptimal conditions. Speed, agility, and mobility are key to modern warfare, but supply chains need to keep up to ensure the warfighters get the ammunition, food, medical, and maintenance tools. To match the pace of forward-deployed soldiers, the 621st Contingency Response Wing (CRW) maintains an alert footing to rapidly create and open airfields domestically and around the globe. The 621st CRW utilizes Air Mobility Liaison Officers (AMLO), who work closely with the Air Force Air

Combat Command (ACC), US Army, and US Marine Corps to deliver critical and relevant supplies to the fight. The 621st CRW has self-sufficient squadrons that can deploy and bring all requirements for airlift, including Port Dawgs, maintainers, air traffic controllers, security forces, and even financers.

While primarily a force projection unit, the 621st CRW provides essential humanitarian aid by enabling critical supplies to flow to disaster areas. Airmen from the 621st CRW participate in relief missions after earthquakes and hurricanes by identifying suitable locations for airfields or drop zones. They have participated in the domestic relief efforts of Hurricanes Irma, Matthew, Maria, and Katrina, while spreading goodwill internationally in recovery operations for earthquakes in Haiti and Pakistan.

The 621st CRW patch has a sun with an olive branch and arrows, meaning they can deliver hope in both peace and war.

Members assigned to the 621st CRW perform security in Mission Oriented Protective Posture gear during an exercise at Travis AFB. (US Air Force photo by Louis Briscese)

Chapter 3

Aircraft

KC-10 Extender

Augmenting the venerable KC-135 Stratotanker fleet are 59 KC-10 Extenders, 27 of which call Travis AFB home. The mission of the KC-10 is to provide fuel in mid-flight to other aircraft. The USAF selected McDonnell Douglas to deliver a total of 60 KC-10s, which is based on the civilian DC-10, and the first models were received in 1981. Some of the reasons the USAF selected the Extender was its ability to take off from shorter runways, nearly 90 percent commonality with the civilian DC-10 enabling easier acquisition of parts, an increase of fuel capacity of nearly 50 percent over the KC-135, and the use of a probe-and-drogue system that can refuel Navy, Marine Corps, and other NATO aircraft.

Powered by three GE CF6-50C2 turbofan engines, the KC-10 produces over 150,000lb of thrust for a maximum unloaded range of 11,500 miles. It can offload over 350,000lb of fuel using its boom or a probe-and-drogue system. The fuel tanks are stored under the floor, where a DC-10 would carry luggage. The Extender is also a capable cargo and passenger transport, able to carry 170,000lb of cargo, such as Humvees and pallets, and up to 75 people. Medical evacuees can also be transported on the KC-10 on patient litters.

A gaggle of KC-10s sit in their parking spots, ready for the next mission. There are 27 total Extenders at Travis AFB.

The KC-10 can support US Air Force, Navy, Marines, and NATO aircraft with its boom and drogue system and can refuel three aircraft at a time.

Only 60 KC-10s were produced, and one was lost to an accident. The remaining 59 are split between Travis and McGuire AFBs.

The refueling boom is controlled by the aircraft's boom operator, who sits in the aft of the aircraft and uses a joystick to move the boom. The boom operator is also in direct communication with the recipient pilot, and the two work as a team to ensure the fuel flows safely and efficiently. The boom operator is also constantly talking to the pilots for efficient crew resource management. A general rule of aviation is to not allow anything to touch their aircraft while it is in flight, yet these skilled professionals intentionally link up their aircraft while transferring highly flammable liquids during aerial refueling. There is intense pressure to get it right on the first try, because any delay in refueling may endanger the next aircraft in line if they are critically low on fuel. Fortunately, the men and women who fly on the KC-10 train hard to ensure mission success.

Serving honorably since the 1980s, the KC-10 fleet is slated for retirement to be replaced by the KC-46A Pegasus. Currently, the Extenders are based only at Travis AFB and McGuire AFB, but several Extenders from McGuire have already headed for the Boneyard at Davis-Monthan AFB, where they will be used for spare parts and scrapped. During McGuire's transition to the KC-46, Travis has been stepping up missions to the eastern United States, providing coverage in the interim. Throughout its storied career, the KC-10 flew with the USAF and Royal Netherlands Air Force, and its civilian equivalents DC-10/MD-10 have been a part of over 50 airlines worldwide. Civilian operators have also begun drawdowns of the DC-10/MD-10, and soon only a handful of aircraft will remain in service, mostly for aerial firefighting purposes. As a result, spare parts and industry support will no longer be available, making the KC-10 retirement a timely decision. Although the end of the road for the KC-10 looms near, for over 40 years the Extender and its crews have given the USAF dependable refueling, cargo lift, and passenger transport, projecting American airpower and helping people around the globe.

Travis KC-10s are normally responsible for West Coast missions, but recently have been covering the East Coast as McGuire transitions to the KC-46.

Note that the wheels turn sideways to fit inside the wheel well of KC-10 serial 87-0123 after takeoff. This maximizes space for cargo and fuel.

The KC-10 can offload a maximum of 1,100 gallons per minute from its six fuel tanks, four in the belly and two in the wings.

Up, up, and away! Travelling at a speed of up to 619mph, this Extender is on its way to meet a thirsty customer.

KC-10 serial 83-0078 taxies out onto the Travis runway. The large door aft of the "U.S. AIR FORCE" insignia opens up to the cargo bay.

At the end of the runway, a KC-10 turns around and gets ready to face downrange for takeoff.

Cleared for takeoff! Three GE F103 engines spool up for maximum power as this KC-10 gets ready to "slip the surly bonds of earth."

The power of the GE F103 engines is apparent in this photo, as water on the runway is turned into mist by over 150,000lb of thrust.

The KC-10 can takeoff with almost twice the weight of a KC-135, prompting some Extender crews to call themselves the "bigger brother" of the refueling community. Needless to say, the KC-135 crews do not agree.

There are four crewmembers on board the KC-10: aircraft commander, copilot, flight engineer, and boom operator/loadmaster. The flight engineer controls the flow of fuel from the flight deck, while the boom operator makes sure the connection to the recipient jet is done safely.

KC-10 85-0031 extends its boom to show its capability to safely and efficiently offload fuel.

Different mechanisms in the boom allow for significant play during refueling. Crews on both the KC-10 and receiving aircraft practice constantly to make sure they are ready to answer the call.

The KC-10 is sometimes referred to as a "three-holer tanker" in reference to the number of engines.

The box on the right is a generator, officially known as a ground power cart, which provides external power to the KC-10. The KC-10 can provide its own power on board with batteries, but while on the ground, the ground power cart helps preserve the batteries.

Two Humvees can fit inside the cargo bay of the KC-10. It takes skill and some creative movements to get them through the door, but a good Port Dawg can get the job done.

The boom operator has two joysticks, one to move the boom itself and the other to move the flight control surfaces. This provides greater control and precision during refueling.

No Bounds! Travis Extenders make sure they can live up to their unit's motto by enabling USAF aircraft to fly all over the world.

C-17 Globemaster III

One of the most versatile aircraft in the USAF inventory is the Boeing C-17A Globemaster III. It can perform a large variety of missions including cargo airlift, paratroop airdrops, and medical evacuations. The C-17 can perform all these missions while only needing 3,500ft of runway (the C-5, in comparison, requires a minimum of 6,000ft), and it can even land on some austere fields. This opens up more runways for use for the C-17, meaning it can be deployed at more locations, projecting American airpower across the globe. According to some USAF studies, the C-17 has the ability to land at over 9,900 airfields around the world, including Antarctica, making the entire planet accessible to the USAF.

Four massive Pratt & Whitney F117-PW-100 engines give the Globemaster III over 160,000lb of thrust, pushing the C-17 to a maximum speed of 450 knots and a service ceiling of 45,000ft with an unrefueled range of 2,400 miles. The C-17 can carry over 170,000lb of cargo or airdrop 102 fully armed paratroopers to the battle zone. The most recent use of airdrops was in Iraq in 2003, in which over 1,000 paratroopers from the 173rd Airborne Brigade were dropped from 15 C-17s to take an airfield at Bashur. After the airfield was secured, additional C-17s were able to ferry in heavy armor. The C-17 also participates in the aeromedical evacuation, with the ability to fly with over 80 patients and their attending medical personnel.

The C-17 is currently used by eight other air forces, including the Indian Air Force and Royal Air Force. Originally designed to replace the venerable C-130 Hercules (the C-130 can never be replaced!), the C-17 eventually filled the airlift role previously held by the C-141 Starlifter. Although the USAF initially ordered 120 C-17s, its success prompted the order to be increased to 223 total aircraft, 13 of which reside at Travis AFB. Built with maintenance in mind, the C-17 requires only 20 man-hours of maintenance for every one hour of flight, meaning the Globemaster III spends less time in the shop and more time in the air completing its missions.

Blast off! C-17 07-7172 jets away from the Travis runway after a touch-and-go landing.

A Travis sunrise is made even more beautiful by a Globemaster III waiting on the ramp.

Affectionately known as the "Moose," C-17s make a distinctive sound when being refueled, which sounds like the mating call of a female moose. Instead of the traditional "elephant walk," a formation of C-17s that taxi and get ready to take off is known as a "moose walk."

Although not as colorful as the nose art of old, the badges on C-17 06-6158 are just as inspiring and provide motivation to the aircrew

Winglets on the C-17, seen on the tips of the wings, increase aerodynamic efficiency by blocking the wingtip vortices from pushing down on the wing, which increase drag by pulling the lift vector backwards. Some studies show up to a 5 percent savings on fuel with the winglets, and over the course of the 27,000 flight hours that Travis performs in a year, the savings add up quickly!

"Exhaust jellies" are seen here, as the gases produced by the engines distort the air behind them. Also seen are rain particles being pulverized into mist by the thrust.

The two strakes seen under the rear fuselage provide additional yaw stability at low speeds or high angles of attack when airflow to the tail is blocked.

Two fins flank each engine, which act as vortex generators and make sure that there is adequate airflow over the wings, delaying stalls at high angles of attack.

The wings on the C-17 are swept back at 25-degree angle, and all flight surfaces retain this angle.

This C-17 is practicing landing on the assault strip. Reverse thrusters help shorten the roll distance needed to land and also enables the aircraft to go backwards while taxiing. The reverse thrusters deflect air upwards, enabling the C-17 to have its engines spooled up while on the ground, so cargo can be unloaded, and the aircraft can take off immediately.

Aside from the typical transport missions, Travis C-17s also provide support to the President's entourage and Thunderbirds aerial display team by hauling much of their associated cargo.

Instead of a traditional yoke used to steer large aircraft, the C-17 utilizes a fighter-esque joystick, as it is exceptionally nimble for an airplane of its size.

No flight engineer is necessary on board the C-17, since it is a "flying computer that will tell you what the problem is with the aircraft," according to Captain McNatt, so there are only three crew members on board: pilot, copilot, and loadmaster.

Left: The "slime lights" are visible on the sides of the fuselage and the winglet, seen here as yellow strips. These are used during formation flying at night, and their brightness can be adjusted.

Below: This C-17 sits in a 60th AMXS maintenance hangar where it is undergoing routine service. The red cylinders on the ceiling release foam to help fight fires that break out inside the hangar.

Right: Starting with the C-17A Block 13 models, Boeing has installed additional internal fuel tanks, seen here with yellow straps around it. Informally, these models are labelled C-17 ER, for "extended range" and provide an additional 400 miles of range.

Below: Paratrooper drops are not usually done by Travis C-17s, although they do retain the ability to perform this mission. The static line mechanisms and green/red lights are still onboard in case the Travis mission changes.

C-5M Super Galaxy

All hail the king of transports! The Lockheed Martin C-5M Super Galaxy is the largest aircraft in the USAF inventory, in both physical size and amount of payload carried. As tall as a six-story building, this massive aircraft can seemingly transport the entire US military arsenal. When the C-5 is taking off, the entire city of Fairfield knows, as its distinctive buzzing engines and deafening roar are impossible to ignore. In 2021, a C-5 even carried two CH-47 Chinooks from the United States to Australia.

Delivering a jaw-dropping 205,000lb of thrust, four General Electric F-138-G100 engines power up to 281,000lb of cargo to a maximum speed of 500mph for over 2,000 miles unrefueled. While first delivered to the USAF in 1970, the C-5 has undergone multiple modernization upgrades since then, which have provided improved engines, avionics, radar, safety, and communications equipment. Both forward and aft ends of the aircraft can open up, enabling more efficient onloading and offloading capabilities. Twenty-eight large nitrogen-filled Goodyear tires support the maximum takeoff weight of 840,000lb. Spanning 121ft, the cargo hold of the C-5 is longer than the Wright Flyer's first flight, showing how far flight has come since the days at Kitty Hawk.

The ability to transport bulky items is the bread and butter of the C-5 and its crew. Heavy equipment that would normally need to be transported over water can instead be moved rapidly by air and also be offloaded faster than at a traditional seaport. Clearly, this has major force projection implications, as combat vehicles and aircraft can be deployed at a moment's notice around the world. The Super Galaxy plays an important part in maintaining global security by providing warfighters with the equipment they need to accomplish their missions.

A pair of C-5Ms wait on the ramp for their next mission. Travis has 26 C-5s in their inventory, ready to tackle any cargo mission.

As the largest plane in the USAF inventory, the C-5 dwarfs the KC-10s behind it. For 15 years, the C-5 was the biggest aircraft in the world until it was surpassed by the An-124 Condor.

Overall, the C-5 has a similar configuration to the C-141 Starlifter, with its four engines and high wing, and is considered its "big brother."

The C-15 has five sets of landing gears, one under the nose and four under the wings, for a total of 28 150lb tires. The skilled maintenance airmen at Travis can change a tire in under 15 minutes.

Although the C-5A/B Galaxies performed admirably during the Gulf War, its mission reliability was significantly less than desirable and, in 1999, a modernization program began, eventually converting all C-5s to the M-model by 2017.

On January 8, 2004, a C-5 taking off from Baghdad International Airport was hit by a shoulder-launched surface-to-air missile in the number four engine. Shrugging off the hit, the C-5 landed safely and was back in service by March, showing the ruggedness of the C-5.

A C-5M towers over this seemingly tiny lieutenant. A unique feature of the C-5 is that the nose cone can open up, and with the rear ramp simultaneously open, cargo can be offloaded and onloaded much more rapidly than with just a rear ramp.

The power of the 200,000lb of thrust is seen in this image as water on the runway is sprayed into the atmosphere. The engines have actually been derated from 60,000lb each to 50,000lb because the airframe is unable to handle the stress.

The heat from the exhaust distorts the view of the hills behind Travis as this C-5 lifts off from the runway.

Cleared for takeoff! The noise of a C-5 on takeoff is deafening and hearing protection is a must when on the flightline. The buzzing sound of the engines is unmistakable.

Fully loaded, a C-5 needs about 8,000ft of runway to get airborne. This C-5 is departing from runway 21R.

The C-5M can fly for 14 hours without being refueled while carrying significant cargo. As a result, it has set over 80 aviation world records in its category, including time to climb with a payload.

The C-5s used to do paratrooper drops, but it was found that opening the doors would create too much stress on the airframe, so that mission was relegated to the C-17 and C-130.

This C-5 is practicing its touch-and-go landings. A C-5 requires a minimum of 6,000ft for landing.

The wheels of the C-5 twist when they are retracted in order to maximize space efficiency. There is a complex system of gears and motors to help move the landing gear.

The silver panel with the hole on the lower fuselage is the exhaust for the auxiliary power unit (APU). The APU provides power to start up the engines, as well as air conditioning, while the aircraft is on the ground, a feature the authors were thankful for while touring the C-5.

The C-5 is sometimes referred to as the FRED, for Fantastically (others use a more colorful term) Ridiculous Economic Disaster, due to procurement issues and high maintenance costs, but the M-model has significantly reduced repair costs.

Like the C-17, the C-5 has a wing sweep of 25-degrees for maximum aerodynamic efficiency and lift.

There are several AN/AAR-47 missile warning systems (MWS) on the C-5 that automatically discharge flares. This image shows the flare dispensers that are tied into the MWS. Additionally, the C-5 has several large aircraft infrared countermeasures systems (LAIRCM) to confuse incoming missiles.

The cargo capacity of the C-5 is unmatched, as it can hold two Chinook helicopters, three Apache or Blackhawk helicopters, or two M-1 Abrams tanks. Travis C-5s practice helicopter movements at least once a year.

This image was taken on top of the C-5 viewport. The flight engineer will climb a ladder to spot for the pilots as the aircraft is taxiing. Two other C-5s and two of the powerful engines are seen here.

KC-46A Pegasus

Looking to the future, Travis AFB will receive 24 KC-46A Pegasus aircraft, which will replace all of the KC-10s on base. The first delivery is scheduled for July 2023 and the final KC-46 will arrive in 2025. To integrate the KC-46 into Travis, a Program Integration Office Team, spearheaded by Lieutenant Colonel Theo Fisher, is actively working to transition to the Pegasus. Chief among their properties is to construct a giant three-bay maintenance hangar, which will be able to accommodate KC-46s and any other aircraft in the AMC inventory, except the massive C-5, which is too large to fit inside. Lieutenant Colonel Fisher of the KC-46 Program Integration Office Team explained that the hangar "is designed to enclose three KC-46 Pegasus aircraft providing our maintainers with major repair capabilities not otherwise possible in outdoor flightline operations. Additionally, the facility will be equipped with modern amenities such as an overhead fall restraint system, KC-46 boom repair station, and wing aerial refueling pod overhaul and storage areas." The 660th and 749th AMXS will maintain the Travis KC-46s.

Based on the Boeing 767 airliner, the KC-46 is a multi-role tanker with the ability to provide air-to-air refueling capabilities for USAF and NATO aircraft and can also fill cargo transport functions. Moving into the realm of science fiction, the KC-46 features an air refueling operator station that has 3-dimensional displays of the refueling process, enabling improved instructions and operations. The KC-46 will have two Pratt & Whitney PW4062 engines, which can put out 62,000lb of thrust each, with a maximum airspeed of 570mph. It can offload over 200,000lb of fuel, hold 65,000lb of cargo, carry 58 passengers, and transport 18 pallets. Like the KC-10, the Pegasus will be able to airlift patients during aeromedical evacuations. Travis will be leading AMC's West Coast operations into the future with the Pegasus.

The KC-46A hangar features three bays that can fully contain any AMC aircraft except for the C-5. Additional safety equipment such as built-in fall protection will help maintainers work on the aircraft safely and quickly.

Walsh Construction crewmen weld two column splices during construction of the KC-46A Pegasus three-bay maintenance hangar. (US Air Force photo by Airman 1st Class Alexander Merchak)

Chapter 4

Operations

Control Tower

Keeping a watchful eye over the entire airfield with its 360-degree vantage point is the control tower, which is situated perfectly between Travis' two offset runways. The primary responsibility of the control tower is to ensure the runways are being used safely and appropriately. The tower makes sure Federal Aviation Administration (FAA) rules are followed and creates sequences so that aircraft can land in the correct order. The watch supervisor is the boss in the control tower regardless of rank, and, as control tower supervisor Master Sergeant Noel Foley explained, "what the watch supervisor says, goes. He listens to the others in the tower and makes the final decision if there are any conflicts." Typically, the tower is staffed by four to five members, but that number can fluctuate based on expected traffic. At the base of the tower is the Radar Approach Facility, where over 300 aircraft are monitored daily in a 1,850 square mile area from ground level to 10,000ft. Unfortunately, these radar operators never get to see the aircraft they are controlling, as they are in a semi-dark room without the gorgeous 360-degree views up top.

A large Travis AFB logo emblazons the front of the control tower, informing all incoming aircraft of their location.

Rising over the airfield, the control tower has a 360-degree view of Travis.

This screen helps keep track of air traffic being tracked on radar. The air traffic controllers use it to ensure safe flights.

These airmen are keeping a watchful eye over the Travis airfield. The view screens are equipped with retractable shades to keep out the glare from the sun.

Communicating with other departments is key to safe flight operations, and this radio system enables the air traffic controllers to quickly contact key personnel, including fire and crash rescue personnel.

The control tower responsibilities are divided between ground control and air traffic control. Ground control takes the aircraft from its parking spot to the runway and also keeps track of vehicles. Once the aircraft is near the runway, it is transferred to air traffic control, where they are responsible for the aircraft until it is approximately five miles from the airfield. Air traffic control will also ask outbound aircraft for weather updates to provide better situational awareness. The control tower also helps with instrument approaches. With certain weather criteria, an instrument landing is required using the Instrument Landing System (ILS), which works to calculate glide slope and runway alignment. The control tower works with the pilot and ILS to help guide the aircraft in and turn on lights as needed. Both the tower and pilots constantly practice using the ILS in fair weather conditions so that their skills are sharp when inclement weather occurs.

When the wind speed reaches approximately 30 knots, the tower begins to noticeably sway and those who are not used to the movement tend to get nervous, as they are 60ft above the ground. At 70 knots, the tower is evacuated for safety reasons and air operations are suspended. A catwalk extends around the exterior of the control tower, allowing for an unobstructed view of the base and surrounding hills. While the tower dominates the landscape, the controllers inside stand out in their own way by handling more traffic, both military and civilian, than any other military tower in the United States.

Security Forces: Military Working Dogs

Aggressive, intimidating, loyal, and dedicated are qualities that would typically describe a great warfighter and can also be applied to Travis's furriest members. Known officially as military working dogs (MWDs), these canines can crush any threat their handlers show them. Some of the MWD breeds that Travis has include the German shepherd, Dutch shepherd, Belgian Malinois, Labradors, and even beagles (no combat Chihuahuas, unfortunately). These MWDs are used as a force multiplier to guard assets and sniff for explosives or narcotics, taking a bite out of crime. All Department of Defense (DOD) MWDs go through initial training at Joint Base San Antonio and are then delivered to their bases or posts as needed. When a new MWD comes to Travis, they undergo additional training and upgrades, similar to how an airman fresh from basic training would receive coaching to become

proficient at their new unit. Each MWD costs between US$60,000 to US$80,000 per year to shelter, feed, and train, making each dog a valuable member of their unit.

All those who handle the MWDs start their careers as Security Forces personnel and that is their initial mission. As kennel master Technical Sergeant Daniel DeLeon explains, "Airmen must go through two or three years of training before going to the K9 unit because unleashing a dog is considered a use of force, and we want to make sure those who use that force can apply it correctly." The career path of an MWD airman begins as a handler, who will then advance to trainer and kennel master. Those who wish to become a handler must possess "confidence, mental composure, and be assertive, but not too overbearing as it can shut down the dog," per DeLeon. Airmen must also pass evaluations to ensure they are capable of working with dogs and are also not afraid to get bitten.

Security at Travis is provided by 60th Security Forces Squadron, whose logo signifies its role as protectors of AMC assets.

A military working dog (MWD) grabs hold of a suspect during a training exercise. Great care is taken to ensure the safety of the dog and correct placement of a bite.

This MWD eagerly awaits its next command from its handler.

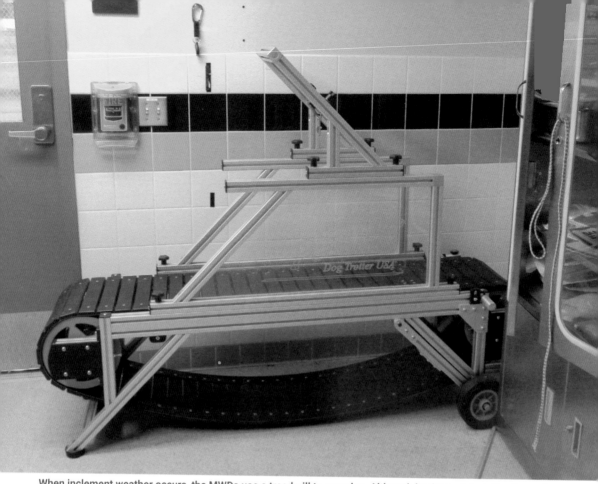

When inclement weather occurs, the MWDs use a treadmill to exercise. Although hesitant at first, the dogs adapt and use this treadmill to stretch their legs.

The equipment room for the handlers shows how much protective gear is required to keep them from serious injuries when training the dogs. Even with this gear, cuts and bruises are common.

The kennels at Travis are a recent addition, having been built in 2013. The current Travis MWD crew consists of four handlers, one trainer, and one kennel master. The veterinarian is a member of the US Army, as are all veterinarians across the DOD, and she is responsible for the health of the dogs. The veterinarian prescribes the diet and medication for the MWDs, but the handlers are able to provide feedback regarding the performance of the dog. For instance, if the veterinarian calls for one serving of food, but the dog's performance decreases, the handler may ask for additional nutrients, and that recommendation is usually enacted. The MWDs and their airmen are a force to be reckoned with, and potential intruders are forewarned about crossing the K9 team.

Security Forces: Phoenix Raven

In keeping with the animal-themed Security Forces, another highly trained and specialized group of airmen are the Phoenix Ravens, who provide security for all AMC aircraft in high-threat areas. Founded in 1997, the Ravens have flown over 2,000 missions to contested airfields around the world. The Ravens' mission is to protect the aircraft and crew to which they are assigned from close-in and local threats. When an AMC asset is headed to an airfield that is not fully secured, a four-man team of Ravens will deploy with the aircraft and report to the aircraft commander. Once on the ground, the Ravens are the first ones off and set up a 360-degree perimeter around the aircraft and ensure the crew is safe. If the need arises for a rapid evacuation, such as receiving small arms fire, Senior Airman Hawley explains that "All aircrew will rally back to the jet, the Ravens will arm up and eliminate the threat. The Ravens will also be the last ones on the jet."

To become a Raven, an airman must first pass the tech school to become a Security Forces officer. When they are assigned to their duty station, such as Travis AFB, they spend a minimum of three weeks preparing for the Ravens training course. Prospective Ravens then spend a month at McGuire AFB in New Jersey learning self-defense techniques, airfield security tactics, and intense physical training. The students are placed under constant stress to simulate battlefield scenarios. For instance, a trainee may be required to perform the Air Force physical fitness test and perform a shooting drill immediately afterward while hitting all required targets. The training is high tempo and tests a candidate's ability to concentrate under stressful situations, but it also ensures the newly minted Raven is up to the task. There are approximately 200 Ravens in the USAF, and approximately 25 of them call Travis home, making them an exclusive and close group.

Although capable of expertly handling firearms, the Ravens use the baton as their primary self-defense weapon. In many countries, carrying a gun is considered taboo, and out of respect for cultural sensitivities, the Ravens only deploy their M-4 rifles and M-9 pistols when absolutely necessary. Therefore, Ravens train extensively with the baton, striking at 45-degree angles and moving to reassess the situation. As part of their training, Ravens learn self-control and to not strike certain areas to prevent serious damage to their opponent including the head, neck, spine, sternum, and groin. Instead, they target the center mass of the arms, legs, and bodies of their opponents to buy time to reevaluate the issue.

Claws extended around a globe, the raven on the logo shows that Phoenix Ravens provide security for AMC around the world.

Above: During a sparring practice with protective gear, the Red Man wears red protective gear while his counterpart strikes with the baton at a 45-degree angle.

Left: Another use of the baton is to push an adversary away, as demonstrated by the airman on the left. This gives the Raven time to reassess the situation and determine their next course of action.

Phoenix Ravens are constantly practicing with and against each other to hone their skills. Although their sparring sessions seem routine and effortless, there is an incredible amount of strength and stamina required to keep up with the Ravens.

Central to the Ravens' ethos is their creed, which they can recite by heart:

Respect for all cultures, I come in contact with ensuring the professional conduct of others and myself as representatives of the United States Air Force.

Achieve through honest endeavor, and persistent effort to do the best under any circumstances.

Volunteer to stand at the forefront of Force Protection, in the defense of deployed assets and personnel for which I am responsible to protect.

Endure the physical hardships of austere environments maintaining the metal tenacity to complete the Raven mission.

Never compromise my position as a Raven, my professional conduct, moral standards, and intestinal fortitude.

Non-Destructive Inspections and Fabrication

Transporting cargo and passengers around the world puts enormous stress on the aircraft that move them. Making sure those forces do not damage the airframes are the dedicated maintenance airmen responsible for performing non-destructive inspections (NDI). Technical Sergeant Sergio Valenzuela

The logo for the Non-Destructive Inspection (NDI) office shows the five types of inspections the shop is capable of performing: X-rays, magnetic testing, fluorescent penetrants, ultrasound, and Eddy currents.

of 60th MXS calls the NDI shop "the radiology department for the aircraft" – an apt description, as he is responsible for using x-rays, magnetic particles, fluorescent penetrants, ultrasound, and electric Eddy currents to find potential structural problems with Travis aircraft. In the coming years, a computed tomography machine, better known as a CAT scan, will arrive at Travis, enabling technicians to generate a 3-dimensional image of a part. The purpose of these tests is to detect cracks or other anomalies without having to cut into the aircraft or otherwise take it apart, saving time and money.

One of the most consistent inspections 60th MXS performs is to check for cracks inside the KC-10 tail. There is a known defect that the aircraft is able to fly with, provided it stays within parameters. This inspection is done every 90 days, and any changes in the status of the structure are immediately reported. Space in this area is limited, so airmen must take care when moving inside the tail section while using portable ultrasound machines for their NDI. The surrounding areas are also inspected to make sure no compensatory stresses are affecting the KC-10. If the gaps become too large, the aircraft is sent in for repairs. The guidelines for the inspection tolerances come from engineers at the research

This contraption is the magnetic testing machine. The suspect part is placed in the middle of the circle and a current is run through it. This produces a magnetic field, and the way the part reacts to the magnetic field is measured and a significant anomaly indicates there may be something wrong with the part.

For the X-ray machine, a part is placed on the table on the target and the X-ray scans it, similar to a dental office. As it is industrial grade, this X-ray machine produces much more radiation than a medical office and requires much more protection for the technician. The concrete walls of this facility are 3ft thick, and the technician is required to stand outside the room.

Ultrasound tests are done with this Epoch 650 portable gauge. It uses sound waves to see inside a part, similar to ultrasounds done in a maternity ward.

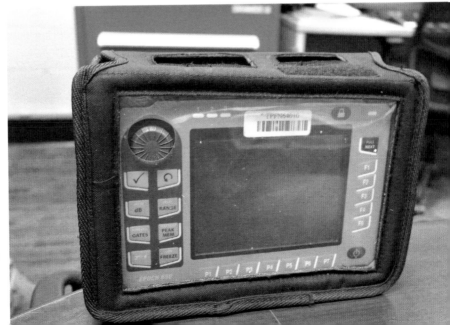

The fabrication shop makes great use out of this 3D printer, which, at the time of this report, was making a very important part for a C-5: the plastic toilet seat! Essential flight components cannot be made in this shop as they must pass Federal Aviation Administration (FAA) approval, but non-essential items can be made en masse here.

In order to mill certain objects, this vertical machining center can be used for die sinking or drilling.

In order to precisely cut through hard materials, a water jet is used, which is faster and more efficient than other traditional forms of cutting, such as sawing.

This computer terminal is the brains for the water jet cutting machine. A program is input into the computer, which tells the water jet the best way to cut a part.

and development levels who decide what deviations are acceptable. Although an invaluable part of the maintenance crew, the NDI technicians are often the bearers of bad news but possess the utmost integrity to point out problems, even if it makes them unpopular. However, the airmen at Travis know the NDI inspections are an important part of having safe flying operations.

Adjacent to the NDI, the fabrication shop possesses a myriad of machines and tools to help create parts for the entire base using wood, metal, and plastic materials. Standard lathes, mills, and presses adorn the shop, but the latest high-tech additions include CNC and 3-D printing machines, and a new metal 3-D printer will arrive at Travis in 2022. Recently, the 60th MXS fabrication shop supported a COVID-19 mission by creating a ramp to help move patients and equipment more easily onto C-17 and C-130 aircraft. They even shipped out the newly made ramps to other bases that were unable to produce their own. The fabrication robot shop stands out as a professional and skilled organization that is able to directly and positively impact the USAF mission.

Explosive Ordnance Disposal

Another group of high-speed Travis airmen is the Explosive Ordnance Disposal (EOD) team, who won AMC's top EOD flight in 2019 and 2020 due to their outstanding performance in readiness exercises. Senior Airman Christopher Waller, an EOD technician, said "EOD has nine mission sets, including supporting conventional munitions operations, aircraft response, counter IED [improvised explosive device] and nuclear responses, UXO [unexploded ordnance] recovery, and other support missions. Because EOD plays a cat-and-mouse game [with the bomb-makers], we study and train to stay ahead of them to prevent them from taking a life." In order to stay current, the EOD team is constantly training to understand how bomb-makers think and what they are capable of building. For example,

Rise of the Machines: the MTRS II robot stands vigilant in front of an EOD bomb suit. The bomb suit weighs a hefty 80lb, and extreme physical fitness is required work in it.

Two dedicated EOD members stand with their robot, suit, gym weights, and battle flags. The EOD gym is stocked with the best equipment so members can perform at their best.

Senior Airman Waller noted that he recently took a class on tactical electronics, which taught him how to identify electrical components in bombs.

In 1944, the Liberty Ship SS *E.A. Bryan* exploded with tons of munitions on board and on the loading pier at Port Chicago in Suisun Bay, killing 322 and wounding 390 more. This disaster launched an untold amount of munitions into Suisun Bay, and to this day, unexploded ordnance continues to wash up on the shores of the Bay Area. The Travis EOD team is duty-bound to investigate these explosives and answers over 100 calls per year. Because of the Port Chicago disaster, the EOD team is one of the busiest in the USAF, but the high volume of calls keeps the EOD team sharp. Other common items the team works with are washed up Coast Guard flares and old war treasures such as grenades. When these conventional munitions are found, the EOD team will find a safe place in the local area to detonate them to avoid transporting dangerous items. Nearly every item found is X-rayed by EOD, who err on the side of caution on every call. Safety is extremely important to all EOD members, and "cowboy tactics" made popular by *The Hurt Locker* movie are reckless and would not be employed by the responsible Travis team.

An unquestioningly loyal member of the team is the Man Transportable Robot System (MTRS) II robot, which is sent out to investigate a suspected IED. The robot helps the team plan for the explosive and provides a first look and reconnaissance for the team leader, who then decides whether or not to don the famous EOD suit and move closer to the target. Made from 80lb of Kevlar, the EOD suit is a blast suit designed to withstand the pressure wave and fragmentation of a nearby explosive. In order to complete the mission while in the suit for extended periods of time, EOD team members must maintain a high degree of physical fitness, which they accomplish by doing daily physical training for at least one hour and using the Air Force's Tier 2 test to measure their capabilities (for reference, the author scored an "Excellent" on the regular Air Force Fitness Assessment but was unable to pass the Tier 2 test).

Although a tough and dangerous job, the Travis EOD team has no shortages of volunteers vying for a spot. When asked why he would work in a high-risk occupation, Senior Airman Waller answered, "I want to push myself to be the best I can be and to be part of a brotherhood. Everyone here is like family, and we're all close to each other." Since the Global War on Terror began, 20 USAF EOD team members have been lost, and their sacrifices have not been forgotten by Travis EOD. Their reputation as elite airmen in the USAF is well earned.

Fuels

If the hard-working airmen are the heart and soul of Travis, then Jet A fuel is the life blood of the base. Pumping this blood throughout the base are the airmen in charge of the petroleum, oil, and lubricants (POL) shop, which supplies all the fuel to the Travis aircraft, including the fuel that is offloaded by the KC-10s. Pipelines run from the fuel dumps underneath the tarmac feeding hydrants at strategic points on the runway, and with the right fuel truck, Technical Sergeant Samuel Wood, who is a POL supervisor, says his airmen "can provide everlasting fuel to the AMC aircraft." Travis utilizes Jet A fuel, which is similar to JP-8 fuel, but with a higher freezing point, and most aircraft in the USAF inventory use Jet A (a notable exception is the U-2 spy plane). Although the exact volume of fuel stored on base is classified, there are at least one million gallons of Jet A at Travis. The fuels received are tested for purity and quality at the POL lab to ensure the aircraft will be able to perform at their best. One such test includes checking the conductivity of the fuel to prevent static build up and discharge while the liquid sloshes around during flight. Another duty of the POL lab is to test the fuels after an accident to determine if the fuel caused a problem in flight.

Helping the airmen refuel the aircraft are four vehicles: C-300, R-11, R-12, and HYMORE fuel trucks, each with a unique capability. The C-300 can hold 1,200 gallons of fuel and is used primarily for

The R-11 fuel truck is the USAF's primary mobile fueling truck, replacing the R-9 in 1989.

The R-12 truck uses a pump system and hydrants along the ramp to push fuel through to aircraft at a rate of up to 1,000 GPM.

ground fueling. The R-11 truck is the most used fuel truck at Travis and holds 6,000 gallons of Jet A. Utilizing the hydrants on the tarmac is the R-12, which is a pump truck that brings the fuel from the underground piping into the aircraft. A hybrid between the R-11 and the R-12 is the HYMORE fuel truck, which can hold 6,000 gallons and also pump fuel from the hydrants. The hydrant trucks can offload up to 1,200 gallons per minute (GPM) and the R-11 can pump 600 GPM, but, given the high fuel capacities of the AMC aircraft, it can take upwards of 45 minutes to top them off, even at these high pump rates. A difficult and arduous task happens when the POL crew have to remove fuel from an aircraft because of maintenance issues or a mission change, which can take all day. Despite the tough job these airmen and their 29 fuel trucks have, they are dedicated to keeping the fuel flowing throughout the base and on aircraft.

An impressive fleet of R-11s waits for thirsty aircraft to order their fill of Jet A fuel.

These R-12s sit ready for their next mission with the KC-46 hangar under construction. The R-12s will no doubt be filling up the KC-46s when they arrive at Travis.

Liquid oxygen tanks are kept on base to provide pure breathing air for aircrews. The tanks are kept on concrete pads instead of asphalt to prevent oxygen from soaking into the oil-filled asphalt and potentially causing an explosion.

These ports refuel the mobile trucks through the top. A truck will park under the spigots and receive Jet A fuel to distribute to the aircraft.

There are four pumping stations throughout Travis, which move fuel from the main storage tanks to either the mobile trucks or the hydrants on the runways.

Areas around liquid gases are kept as clean as possible to avoid contamination and safety issues.

Having finished offloading its fuel, this R-11 poses in front of its handiwork: a quenched C-5 Galaxy.

Liquid nitrogen is used to fill tires as well as suppress fires in fuel tanks by displacing oxygen.

An R-11 is on its way to provide Jet A to a thirsty flightline.

The petroleum, oil, and lubricants (POL) team is the lifeblood of Travis: no one flies without them. One of the main fuel storage tanks is visible on the left.

A unique and tangentially related responsibility for the POL team is the distribution and testing of nitrogen and oxygen gases. Nitrogen is used for fire suppression in fuel tanks to displace oxygen in the event of a fire and is also utilized in filling tires. In order to deliver breathable air to the flight crew, the POL shop also provides 99.5 percent oxygen, which is tested for purity and odor. Both the nitrogen and oxygen are stored as liquid in tanks in a remote area of the base so that they are isolated and do not endanger sensitive equipment. Higher USAF leadership have called upon Travis' unique capabilities in being able to handle liquid fuels and gases to test new processes and equipment for the wider USAF mission. Because of their skill and leading-edge training, Travis POL airmen are at the tip of the spear in their career field.

Air Mobility Liaison

A unique mission to the Air Force is the Air Mobility Liaison Officer (AMLO) and its enlisted counterpart, the Expeditionary Air-Ground Liaison Element (EAGLE). The AMLO is a rated Air Mobility pilot and is a special joint-development assignment that lasts approximately two to three years. The AMLO is fundamentally embedded with an Army about 80 percent of the time, and their job is to integrate the air and ground components by translating Air Force and Army languages. Participating in some Army training, the AMLO ensures they are able to participate with their unit in limited engagements, including combat skills training. Both the AMLOs and EAGLEs are a part of the 621st CRW, which is co-located at Travis AFB and Joint Base McGuire. Although no active AMLOs are currently stationed at Travis, the base has supported and trained for the mission while hosting former AMLOs and using their experience to continue air mobility operations.

A core mission of the AMLO is to assist paratrooper operations. During NATO exercise Swift Response 2021, the 173rd Airborne Brigade jumped into Bulgaria from C-17s and, on the very first aircraft, right next to the ground-force commander, was an AMLO, immediately getting on radios to coordinate follow-on aircraft and drop zone safety. At the strategic level, the AMLO advises all levels of command, including general officers, as to the capabilities and availability of the AMC. An Army commander will lean on the AMLO to inform them how AMC operations will be able to support Army missions. Conversely, the AMLO will report back to AMC about the importance and requirements of the Army commander, decreasing the adversity and friction between the two groups. Higher level army commanders, including generals, will ask AMLOs to validate their war plans such as availability and capacity of certain aircraft, integrating the command and control entities between the Army and Air Force.

The EAGLE will assist the Army in their cargo load planning. When an Army commander is planning an exercise and calls for an Air Force transport, the EAGLE will help prepare the cargo to be ready to be loaded onto the aircraft as soon as it arrives, preventing AMC assets from simply idling on the ramp. Delays in cargo loading may affect other missions and scheduling, potentially endangering other important operations. The EAGLEs will train Army personnel in securing and inspecting cargo loads.

In response to the Iranian missile attack on Al Asad Airbase in 2020, the USAF helped deploy missile defenses, including the Avenger, CRAM, and Patriot systems, to three separate airfields in Iraq. Shuttling in these systems was not permitted by the Iraqi government, but AMLOs were placed on the first AMC aircraft to help guide the aircraft in and to clear follow-on forces into Baghdad International Airport. American aircraft were warned about violating Iraqi airspace by Iraqi control towers, but the AMLOs were able to coordinate with the US Central Command (CENTCOM) commander, General McKenzie, and the aircrew to provide clearance to land anyway. Although not typically a mission assigned to AMC, the AMLOs played an integral part in forcibly taking over an international airport.

They also coordinated with Australian and New Zealand Army Corps (ANZAC) special forces and Joint Terminal Attack Controllers (JTACs) to help relay intelligence back to higher commands.

Supporting disaster response is also a major part of the AMLO responsibility. In the event that civilian infrastructure has been knocked out at an airport, AMLOs can take control of the runway and airspace to help coordinate cargo upload and download. Although the contents of the cargo are different, the time, space, capacity, and requirements of AMC aircraft remain the same for either a wartime situation or a natural disaster.

Aeromedical Evacuation

Transporting wounded or sick airmen, sailors, marines, soldiers, and other DOD personnel from forward bases to a higher level of care are the nearly 70 medical professionals of the 60th and 349th AES. According to Major Elizabeth Persico, a nurse with 60th AES, the mission of the AES is to "maintain readiness by keeping up with training and clinical requirements, which allows us to deploy in hours." A typical AES team consists of three technicians and two nurses who will travel with a patient on an AMC aircraft, and they can also work with other specialists including burn units, doctors, and critical care nurses. The 60th and 349th AES are qualified to transport patients on the KC-10, C-17, and C-130, which can accommodate litters and seats as necessary.

With the recent COVID-19 pandemic, the Travis AES team jumped right into the fight and transported some of the first COVID-positive patients from Afghanistan to Rammstein in Germany. In February 2020, when three American civilian contractors in Afghanistan tested positive and were

This negatively pressurized connex (NPC) is designed for use in the C-130. The unit carries its own oxygen, as the aircraft oxygen is not available for patient use.

NPCs rated for the C-17 are staged and ready for the next mission. As seen, the NPC is a conex box that has been converted for medical use.

Before entering the patient area, the medical staff must enter this anteroom to put their gowns on and prepare for treatment. When leaving the patient, this room is used to decontaminate the nurse or technician.

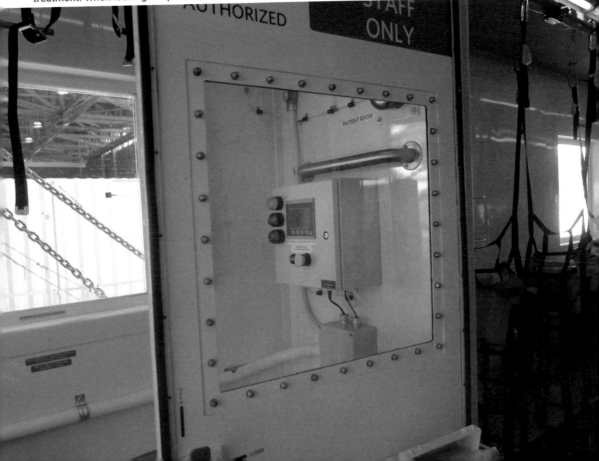

The patient seating areas are surprisingly comfortable, and the storage boxes on the webbing can be used as a makeshift pillow.

required to be transported to Rammstein, Major Persico deployed within 48 hours of getting the initial call. She and her team were able to safely transport the sick contractors to Germany at a time of great uncertainty and changing medical guidance, showcasing her dedication to her profession and patients. A tool that the AES uses is the negatively pressurized conex (NPC), which is a container box that maintains negative pressure to keep the patient isolated. At Travis, there are four NPCs that are rated for use on the C-17 and one smaller NPC for the C-130, and they can hold 30 and 16 people, respectively.

A recent AES mission shows how much the USAF cares for its citizens when it dispatched a team from the 349th to transport a critically ill, COVID-19 positive civilian from Juneau, Alaska, to a higher care facility in San Antonio, Texas. On October 31, 2021, the 349th received a call from higher headquarters to prepare to move a patient who was in a medically induced coma after falling to the effects of COVID-19. Normally, the AES team is given 48 hours' notice, but because this patient was in such critical condition, they were instead given only an hour to deploy. A Travis C-17 was retasked to bring an NPC and the AES team to the patient, and within the day, they had arrived in Alaska and began preparing to receive the patient. By the next day, the patient had been safely moved to a facility in San Antonio that was able to provide the higher level of care required, and the AES team was back at Travis by November 2, 2021. It is an enormous undertaking to utilize the NPC and arrange for a C-17 flight on such a short notice, but it was routine to the dedicated folks at the 349th. Travis airmen can not only support war-time operations, but they also pledge hope and care to those who are gravely ill.

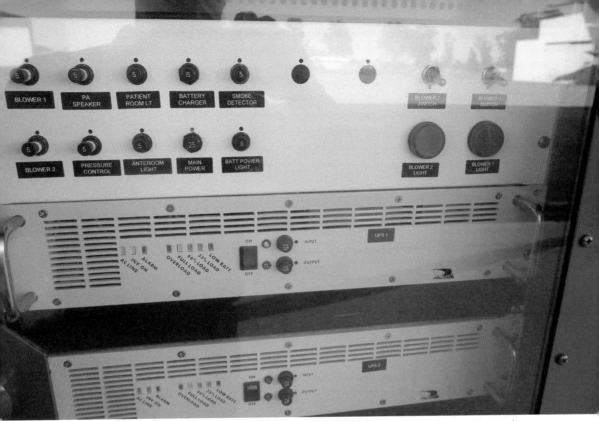

This control panel helps maintain the negative pressure environment needed to keep both the patient and aircrew safe.

This C-17 flew a mission to Alaska, carrying vital COVID-19 equipment including an NPC to help support a civilian mission.

Band of the Golden West

A fun and unusual unit at Travis AFB is the USAF Band of the Golden West, which has about 60 musicians, performing marches, ensembles, and honor guard functions. They have played with world renowned orchestras including the Los Angeles Philharmonic and San Francisco Symphony, while wowing fans of the San Francisco 49ers and Giants at their respective stadiums. The Band of the Golden West helps improve morale through recreational events, supports important functions such as funerals, and tells the Air Force story through music and narration. One of the most important missions of the band is to "build goodwill toward the Air Force and spread patriotism within the audience," according to conductor Major Joe Hansen.

All band members must try out before joining the Air Force. Prospective musicians will reply to a call for auditions and submit a sample of their work, be it CD, DVD, or YouTube link, and those who are qualified are invited for a live recital at Travis. Selections are based on their performance compared to other applicants, and once they accept the offer, they enlist and attend the regular Air Force Basic Military Training (all band members throughout the USAF are enlisted, except for the conductors). There is no technical school or training for the newly minted airmen, as they are expected to be proficient at their craft already. In fact, many of the musicians already have their master's and even doctorate degrees before they join. Per Major Hansen, these airmen are motivated to "serve their country and play music."

Although playing music is their primary duty, all band members have additional responsibilities appropriate to their rank, including managing resources and organizing tryouts, concerts, and other events. Every member practices in some way every day, and Travis has a state-of-the-art recital

The Band of the Golden West is composed of talented musicians, many of whom have graduate degrees. Major Hansen, for instance, holds a doctorate degree in music, and uses his knowledge as the conductor.

Travis has a purpose-built facility for the band, which includes this recital hall with sound attenuation on the walls for better clarity.

The US Air Force Band of the Golden West performs during halftime of the San Francisco 49ers and New York Giants Monday Night Football game at Levi's Stadium in Santa Clara, California, November 12, 2018. The band performed in honor of Veterans Day and to support the National Football League's Salute to Service Campaign. (US Air Force photo by Louis Briscese)

hall and sound booths to help hone their skills. The band is kept busy throughout the year, with an average of 300 performances annually, and their schedule is especially full during patriotic holidays, including Independence Day and Veterans Day. An exciting recent performance that the band attended was the 2022 Rose Bowl Parade, which celebrated the 75th Anniversary of the USAF. The Band of the Golden West marched in the 75th position and joined other Air Force bands to have a total of 75 musicians. Their latest recording, *American Tapestry*, is available in CD form and is available on their Facebook page.

Phoenix Spark

In an effort to reduce costs and increase process efficiency, the Phoenix Spark program was created at Travis AFB. Phoenix Spark teaches any interested airmen how to use computer coding programs and 3-D printers to help shops with rapid prototyping essential parts. Instead of contracting out the design and manufacture of small parts, which could take years of procurement processes, airmen can learn to create their own parts that are unique to their jobs and can provide results in a matter of days. This helps speed up solutions while saving money during the contracting phases. A brilliant example of Phoenix Spark helping warfighters occurred during the evacuation of Kabul. A Travis AFB C-17 pilot noticed that with the large number of refugees, the bathroom facilities were insufficient because the bladders holding waste were not large enough. The pilot asked Phoenix Spark to come up with a part that could transfer the waste from the on-board urinals to a larger tank. Within 20 hours, that part was on its way to Afghanistan, an unheard-of turnaround time.

Phoenix Spark is looking to add to its repertoire of functions by applying lessons learned from rapid prototyping of physical parts to making processes more efficient, cutting through unnecessary bureaucracy. Some areas that Phoenix Spark is making headway in are workflow assignments and ordering commercial parts. This involves testing out multiple types of software at a small-scale level and finding which ones are most appropriate and effective. Instead of going with a single large contractor that may not pan out, Phoenix Spark has suggested that a better way to contract is to go with many smaller bids to find what works and then providing a larger follow-on contract to those who can handle the job. This saves the Air Force time and money by not having to deal with underperforming contractors, but still provides valuable experience to those who are not accepted for the final delivery.

Travis AFB was a natural choice to start Phoenix Spark because of its proximity to Silicon Valley, as well as its innovative airmen. Home to some of the most prestigious universities and companies, the Bay Area's entrepreneurial spirit carries over to the nearby Phoenix Spark program, which routinely hosts industry leaders and experts to help inspire and connect with young airmen. Another reason for Phoenix Spark's success is the fact that Travis is able to support the program, with both financial and intellectual resources. Of course, none of these factors matter without buy-in from top leadership, and fortunately, senior officers have provided the necessary backing to enable this cutting-edge initiative.

Chapter 5

Evacuation of Kabul

Although the AMC does not receive front-page recognition for its role in the Global War on Terror, the airmen at Travis AFB had a direct and actionable impact during the evacuation of Kabul in 2021, known as Operation *Allies Refuge*. Seven out of Travis' 13 C-17s were deployed to the relief effort and evacuated over 7,000 refugees in two and a half weeks. Captain Heather McNatt of 349th AMXS explained that their C-17s were able to extract 500 to 600 refugees each with the help of extended range fuel tanks above the cargo area. Although not its primary mission, Travis KC-10 crews showed flexibility and a willingness to contribute to the operation by whisking over 3,300 Americans and Afghans to safety. Staff Sergeant Murray, a KC-10 maintainer, recalled that every space in the cargo area of the KC-10 was filled with empty pallets with two cargo straps over them, and the refugees "sat down and held on for dear life." In total, Travis aircraft flew over 200 sorties, helped more than 10,000 people escape the Taliban, moved 170,000 tons of cargo, and deployed over 350 brave airmen.

Other airmen from Travis contributed to the humanitarian mission. The previously mentioned Ravens provided security for the AMC C-17s that landed at Kabul. Under normal circumstances, a Raven team has three to four members, with at least two providing exterior security and one "shooter" on the aircraft who would be able to render backup in the form of an M-4 rifle and M-9 pistol. During Operation *Allies Refuge*, teams were pared down to two Ravens, all while increasing operational tempo to feverish pace. Seasoned Raven Staff Sergeant McFerran recalls that he flew ten missions in 14 days during his deployment. Not only was he responsible for perimeter security of the C-17 on the ground, he also "provided flight deck denial, and would post security so the refugees wouldn't get to the cockpit." As part of their security responsibilities, the Ravens checked each refugee for white wristbands indicating the person had been properly vetted. When unauthorized people made it to the aircraft, Travis Ravens removed those personnel with the help of additional security forces. On August 16, 2021, a now-viral video surfaced of desperate Afghan refugees crowding a runway at Hamid Karzai International Airport as a C-17 was attempting to take off. Immediately after this incident, Travis Ravens and their US Army escorts were deployed to the airport and were able to restore order and security by August 18, 2021, a testament to their professionalism and training.

Medical personnel from 60th and 349th Aeromedical Evacuation Squadrons were also dispatched to Afghanistan to provide care to refugees and Americans as medics and nurses. Their primary mission is to care for patients while being transported, but their skills as medical professionals were too valuable to be limited to just flights. With AES boots on the ground, the lives of countless Afghans were improved. These professionals endured a high-tempo and ever-changing environment, including airborne childbirths! At the time of writing, personnel were still being debriefed and not all details have been released of their harrowing experiences.

Another group of elite airmen who participated in Operation *Allies Refuge* were the AMLOs, some of whom are part of the 621st CRW at Travis. Although the specifics of their mission remain classified, several AMLOs were on the ground during the evacuation, providing air traffic control coordination and a safe transition after US forces left the area. The AMLOs were able to connect with the 82nd Airborne Division, contingency response forces, and airfield officials to ensure efficient air transport.

As seen from the control tower, these Travis assets stand ready for their next mission. During Operation *Allies Refuge*, all these parking spots were empty, as all hands on deck supported the airlift.

C-17s played an integral role in the evacuation of Kabul by being the primary airlifter of refugees and Americans.

It is difficult to appreciate the sheer magnitude of the airlift capability at Travis. Even from an elevated view, there seems to be an endless landscape of transport aircraft.

Travis KC-10s did more than just refuel aircraft for Operation *Allies Refuge*: they helped move cargo and people as well. Although outside of their mission, KC-10 crews did everything they could to ensure success.

The passenger area of the KC-10 is fairly limited, so the crews had to be resourceful in getting people out. Using pallets and cargo straps as makeshift seatbelts, KC-10 airmen were able to rescue desperate refugees.

Getting all of these aircraft out of Travis and into Afghanistan was no small undertaking, and all airmen who participated both at home and overseas deserve credit and recognition for their efforts.

C-17s received significant media coverage for their role in the Kabul airlift, and for good reason. Their ability to take off and land in suboptimal conditions while carrying a massive amount of weight stood out during Operation *Allies Refuge*.

Sometimes it is easy to be awed by the capabilities of the C-17, but even more potent is the skill and proficiency of the aircrew, which is often overshadowed by the machines. The C-17 is simply the tool used by dedicated airmen to accomplish their mission.

While the C-17s were out, Travis C-5s provided coverage for AMC sorties. The capacity for AMC to support a historic airlift while maintaining other regular operations speaks to the dedication of its airmen.

Operation *Allies Refuge* required all hands on deck from AMC, and Travis aircraft and its crews flew headlong into the relief operation. In order to move all these aircraft safely and efficiently, the control tower kicked into high gear as everyone prepared to deploy. Putting in long and stressful hours, the professionals working ground and air traffic control were able to send all three of Travis' airframes into the operation without incident, showcasing their skills and competency.

Travis airmen served admirably during the evacuation of Kabul and became a part of history, as the airlift was one of the largest airborne operations in history. During Operation *Allies Refuge*, over 120,000 total people were evacuated in just over two weeks and under extreme duress, as the airport itself was under attack, with a terrorist bombing killing 13 American troops, and in danger of being overrun.

While performing a difficult and complicated task, Travis airmen maintained their professionalism and were compassionate to those in distress. The magnitude of their work is worthy of medals and citations, yet the airmen involved remain humble and note that it was an honor to help their country.

Chapter 6
Air Refueling

On a rainy November morning, a C-5M Super Galaxy, registration number 87-0029, thundered its way into the heavens with two grateful journalists on board. The crew was on its way to a refueling track to practice connecting with the boom of a KC-10 Extender. No fewer than four pilots of varying ranks and experiences had the controls of the C-5 at some point during the three-hour flight. A young captain who had never performed an aerial refuel was being instructed how to approach the tanker, while a veteran lieutenant colonel, who was a command pilot, masterfully guided his aircraft to link up with the boom.

Throughout the refueling, the boom operator and pilot were in constant communication with each other while the C-5 copilot offered constant guidance to the aircraft commander. To simulate a more intense and real-world scenario, both aircraft practiced a radio silent contact and emergency breakaway using the pilot director indicator (PDI) lights on the KC-10 for communication. The PDI lights indicated the approach for the C-5, telling the receiving aircraft to pull forward or aft as necessary until contact with the boom was made. To perform a radio silent emergency breakaway, the PDI lights flashed for 10 seconds, and the C-5 descended rapidly to create space between the two aircraft. In a great display of proper crew resource management, all members were able to talk to each other freely and point out potential safety issues. After the refueling, the pilots went through their post-air-refueling checklist, and they began their descent back to Travis. Their professionalism and skill while handling the largest aircraft in the USAF inventory was astounding. Additionally, the enlisted crew members who monitored the aircraft were equally talented and made sure the flight was smooth from takeoff to landing.

A large part of these airmen's time is spent training, because, as Prime Minister Winston Churchill quipped, "when the battle drum beats, it is too late to sharpen your sword." This mission was just one of many flown that day by Travis airmen, as they prepared themselves to answer their nation's call at a moment's notice. When trouble brews halfway around the world, there is no time to train, and basic skill sets must be instinctual. Practicing aerial refueling provides confidence to the airmen and also reassures mission planners that their assets will be available when the time comes. Although training is sometimes tedious, it pays off, and the progression of expertise was evident on this flight: the rookie pilot required significant instruction while the command pilot was able to connect to the boom on the first shot without much input. America's military power stems in part from frequent and realistic training so that the tempo throughout an operation will be too intense for an enemy to counter.

Air refueling operations play a major part in Air Force doctrine. In World War Two, Allied commanders believed strategic bombing into the heart of Germany would be the key to victory. However, after several missions with high losses, including the failed Schweinfurt raid on October 14, 1943, known as Black Thursday, bomber commanders would not allow raids into Germany until a long-range fighter escort became available.[2] The introduction of the P-51 Mustang, which could escort bombers all the way to the target and back, enabled the Allies to continue their bombing campaign and effectively neutralize the Luftwaffe during Big Week, clearing the way for D-Day operations. Air Force leadership realized the importance of having a fighter that was able to escort bombers to their destinations and invested an

---

2. Mets, D. R. *Master of Airpower: General Carl A. Spaatz.* Novato: Presidio Press, pp 196–198 (1988)

Some of the aircrew in the cockpit of the C-5 are pictured here. Those pictured work primarily on the flight deck as pilots and flight engineers.

A KC-10 is framed by the windows and pilot of a C-5. Like most other commercial aircraft, the pilot is in the left seat with the copilot to their right. This seating arrangement dates back to World War Two when the left-hand torque of the propeller engines made turning to port more convenient.

This pilot's steady hands keeps the C-5 in level flight, ready to take on fuel. The flight controls are between the pilot and copilot so that both of them can control the aircraft.

incredible amount of time, money, and lives to develop long-range aircraft. This resulted in some curious airplanes and concepts, including so-called parasite fighters, which could be launched and recovered by mothership bombers, as well as coupling fighters to bombers via wingtip connections.[3] Tragically, some of these experiments proved fatal, as unpredictable vortices and air disturbances caused mid-air collisions.

Fortunately, the development of aerial refueling was able to more safely extend the range of the fighters, who could then provide their necessary escort. Strategic USAF leaders have come to rely on air refueling for planning sorties, as a non-escorted bombing mission would incur unacceptable losses. Air refueling opens the door to additional targets for bombers and reduces friendly casualties. Additionally, it enabled the USAF to present a nuclear deterrent during the Cold War via Operation *Chrome Dome*, in which bombers armed with nuclear weapons loitered 24/7 for eight years just outside of the Soviet Union. Roving bombers guaranteed second-strike capability in the event the Soviet Union knocked out Strategic Air Command bases, thus assuring mutual destruction.

The advantages of having air refueling capabilities are endless. Close air support aircraft can loiter longer over troops in contact, giving them additional fire, and cargo aircraft can be ferried across oceans, which transport supplies more quickly than ships. The tanker community frequently cites the acronym NKAWTG, which stands for Nobody Kicks Ass Without Tanker Gas, a saying supported by over 60 years of USAF refueling capability. Refueling sorties performed at Travis are an integral part of US military doctrine, and their importance cannot be overstated. Friendly forces around the world depend on Travis airmen to keep them fueled up and in the fight.

---

3. Anderson, C. E., Hamelin, J. P., & Yeager, C. *To Fly and Fight: Memoirs of a Triple Ace*. United States: Clarence E. Anderson, pp 238–242 (2018)

The "glass cockpit" was installed in all C-5s as part of their modernization upgrades. Analog displays for the horizon, fuel status, and radar have been replaced by electronic screens, making it easier for the pilots to read and interact with their instruments.

The pilots are in constant communication with each other to ensure proper crew resource management. Regardless of rank, everyone is responsible for safety and copilots are encouraged to speak up to the aircraft commander if something is unsafe.

These flight engineers keep the aircraft flying by monitoring essential systems. The flight engineers also help with navigation and monitoring atmospheric conditions.

A senior instructor pilot sits in the jump seat between the pilots, monitoring their flight and providing input when needed.

From approximately 500ft away, the extended KC-10 boom can be seen, ready to hook up. Although the autopilot can be used to get the C-5 within 200ft of the KC-10, the pilot was encouraged to fly manually the entire way.

This KC-10 is open for business and ready for a thirsty customer!

C-5 pilots use references to gauge how far away they are from the tanker. For instance, if the bottom of the window frame meets with the nose of the KC-10, it means the C-5 is a certain distance from the other aircraft.

The pilots use the yellow stripe to align themselves down the center of the tanker. Indicator lights on either side of the stripe are used by the tanker to communicate the actions the C-5 should take.

The KC-10 has the capability of refueling with a probe-and-drogue system, which is seen to the right of the refueling boom. A hose is extended out and a Navy aircraft can hook up and receive fuel.

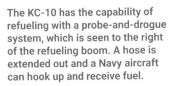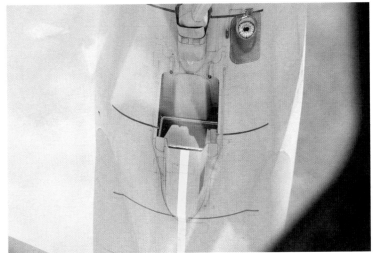

After connecting to the refueling port aft of the cockpit, the pilots can look straight up through the canopy and admire the colorful boom.

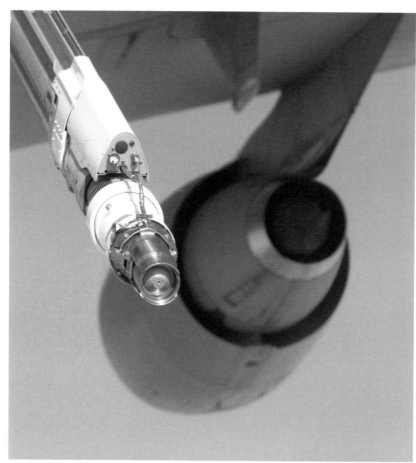

Left: The business end of the refueling boom has locks that hook it into place with the recipient aircraft.

Below: A unique perspective shows the boom operator and his handiwork in the reflection of the window. The boom can be seen plugging into the refueling port.

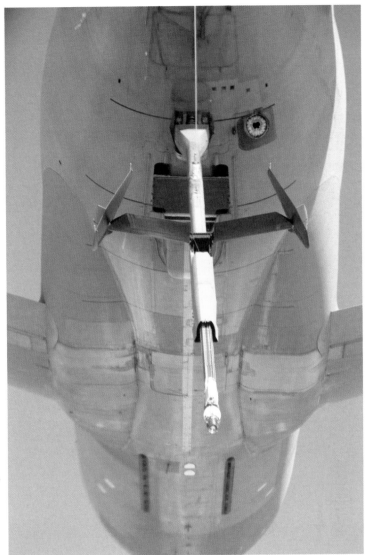

Right: After offloading the required amount of fuel, the KC-10 breaks away and begins to retract its boom.

Below: Another successful mission! After a three-hour mission, both the KC-10 and C-5 return to Travis to refuel and practice takeoffs and landings.

Epilogue

Watching most recruiting commercials would lend a viewer to believe that the USAF is exclusively made up of fighter pilots and special forces airmen, but it is the Air Mobility Command that provides the backbone of not just the Air Force, but all other military branches as well. Without the proper equipment, food, tools, fuel, and weapons, the pilots and other Tier One Special Operations Forces would be unable to execute their missions, and the airmen of the AMC keep them in the fight. One of the biggest contributors to the AMC's capabilities is the airmen and aircraft at Travis Air Force Base. Its nickname "Gateway to the Pacific" is a well-earned moniker, and it provides logistical support to America's force projection not just in Asia, but across the globe as well.

The unsung heroes at Travis are essential to supporting not only the military effort but also humanitarian aid to those in need. Evidenced by their willingness to jump into the fight against COVID-19, Travis airmen are completely dedicated to helping their fellow countrymen in times of peace and war. Americans can be proud of the herculean efforts of these airmen and should rest assured that no matter the situation, Travis AFB will answer the call to defend freedom and make the world a better place.

As seen in this head on shot, the KC-10 can be refueled in midair itself. The markings on top of the cockpit guide the boom into the refueling port.